THE 8C APPRAISAL FRAMEWORK

For Professional and Personal Growth

Written by

Mr. Dimpu Sarath Kumar and Mr. Sai Gupta

Title: *The 8C Appraisal Framework*

Written by: *Mr. Dimpu Sarath Kumar and Sai Gupta*

Disclaimer:

The 8C Appraisal Framework is intended solely for educational, developmental, and inspirational purposes. The concepts, interpretations, and strategies presented are original insights designed to enhance self-awareness, performance, and personal growth. This book does not offer psychological, medical, or legal advice, and readers are encouraged to apply the principles thoughtfully within their individual contexts. Any resemblance to real-life situations or individuals is purely coincidental. The authors and publisher assume no responsibility for outcomes based on the application of the content.

First Edition: 2025

TABLE OF CONTENTS

PREFACE

In a world shaped by rapid transformation and continuous change, the need for a structured yet adaptable approach to personal and professional development has never been more essential. The 8C Appraisal Framework was created with this purpose in mind. It blends timeless values with practical strategies that can be applied across education, employment, and everyday life. This book emerged from a simple but powerful question: How can we help individuals, institutions, and organizations grow with clarity, purpose, and resilience? Our journey led us to identify eight key components that influence meaningful growth. These became the foundation of the framework; Communication, Configuration, Chronicle, Completeness, Conception, Cognizance, Comprehensive Thinking, and Case Study Analysis. Each chapter in this book explores one of these eight components, connecting theory with practice.

The 8C Appraisal Framework is not a rigid set of rules. Instead, it is a flexible guide that encourages reflection, promotes personal responsibility, and supports continuous improvement. This book is an invitation to look beyond the surface, align with your purpose, and take the next step with confidence.

With sincerity and purpose,

Dimpu Sarath Kumar & Sai Gupta

ACKNOWLEDGMENT

With deep gratitude, we extend our heartfelt thanks to everyone who made *The 8C Appraisal Framework* a reality. This book is the result of a vision nurtured by learning, collaboration, and belief in the power of growth.

We sincerely thank our families for their unwavering support and patience throughout this journey. Their encouragement gave us strength through every challenge and inspiration in every breakthrough.

To our mentors, educators, and colleagues, thank you for shaping our thinking, sharpening our insights, and constantly pushing us to strive for excellence.

A special note of appreciation to the team at Intern Stump, whose commitment and creativity have brought this idea to life. Your dedication made each chapter more meaningful, practical, and impactful.

Finally, to our readers; students, educators, professionals, and lifelong learners; this book is for you. May these 8Cs empower your journey and spark transformation in every path you walk.

With gratitude,
Dimpu Sarath Kumar & Sai Gupta

INTRODUCTION TO THE 8C APPRAISAL FRAMEWORK

For Personal and Professional Excellence

In a rapidly evolving world defined by complexity, competition, and innovation, the demand for excellence extends beyond academic brilliance or corporate proficiency. Whether it is a student preparing for future careers, an employee navigating the challenges of a dynamic workplace, a teacher fostering the growth of young minds, or an organization striving for sustainable success, a structured framework that promotes all-round development is essential. The 8C Framework offers such a structure. It encapsulates eight pivotal dimensions: Communication, Configuration, Chronicle, Completeness, Conception, Cognizance, Comprehensive, and Case Study Analysis. These dimensions serve as guiding principles for continuous learning, performance assessment, decision-making, and meaningful contribution.

Evolution of the 8C Framework: The 8C Framework is the result of intensive observation, educational practice, and behavioral studies that aim to bring out the full potential in individuals and institutions. Each component of this framework has evolved through practical experience and theoretical insights, forming a unified model that can be applied across diverse environments. It bridges gaps in learning, performance measurement, strategy execution, and personal development.

While many frameworks exist in silos, addressing only educational pedagogy or corporate training, the 8C Framework operates at the intersection of these domains. It is designed to empower five core audiences: students, employees, organizations, people from various walks of life, and teachers who are responsible for assessing and mentoring others. Through the following chapters, we shall explore the distinct yet interconnected roles of each C and how they influence behavior, productivity, and growth across multiple spheres.

1. Communication: The Pulse of Progress: Communication is the foundation of every human interaction. For students, it is not only about expressing ideas but also about understanding instructions, collaborating with peers, and presenting thoughts clearly in academic settings. Employees, on the other hand, rely heavily on effective communication to perform tasks, attend meetings, resolve conflicts, and contribute to organizational goals.

For organizations, communication structures determine the flow of information and the speed of decision-making. A well-defined communication culture ensures that all stakeholders remain aligned. For teachers, communication is a powerful tool for instruction, motivation, and evaluation. Effective teachers cultivate communicative competence among students and model the behavior expected in professional settings.

In general life, individuals who master the art of communication can navigate social situations more effectively, create stronger relationships, and advocate for their needs. Within the 8C Framework, communication is not limited to verbal expression but extends to listening skills, written correspondence, and digital fluency. It is a core enabler for all other competencies.

2. Configuration: The Blueprint of Efficiency: Configuration refers to the ability to arrange, structure, and optimize resources, tasks, and processes. For students, this means managing study schedules, organizing learning materials, and customizing learning approaches. It also includes configuring digital tools to enhance productivity.

Employees engage in configuration when they set up work systems, create reports, or optimize workflows to achieve better outcomes. Organizations apply configuration in structuring teams, developing strategic plans, and managing technological infrastructures.

People, in their daily lives, configure routines, budgets, and even relationships to create balanced lifestyles. Teachers apply configuration by planning lesson modules, classroom activities, and assessment strategies that cater to diverse learning styles.

The concept of configuration teaches that success is not accidental but the result of deliberate planning and structured execution. Within the 8C Framework, configuration ensures that goals are pursued with methodical precision.

3. Chronicle: The Power of Reflective Record-Keeping: Chronicle emphasizes the value of documenting experiences, thoughts, progress, and outcomes. For students, journaling academic efforts, maintaining portfolios, or keeping a record of achievements fosters self-awareness and accountability. It also helps in revisiting past work to recognize patterns and improve future efforts.

Employees benefit from chronicle through activity logs, project diaries, or performance journals that serve as evidence of growth and learning. Organizations maintain chronicles through reports, data records, and operational logs that guide future decisions.

For individuals, chronicling life events supports mental clarity and goal alignment. Teachers who maintain observation journals can offer deeper insights during student assessments and improve teaching strategies. This dimension instills the habit of reflection, which is key to self-improvement.

Chronicle transforms scattered actions into structured narratives, allowing stakeholders to track evolution, understand mistakes, and celebrate milestones. It acts as a mirror for introspection within the 8C system.

4. Completeness: The Essence of Excellence: Completeness is the practice of finishing tasks with accuracy, responsibility, and attention to detail. For students, this means not just submitting assignments but ensuring that work meets the expected standards and learning objectives.

Employees exhibit completeness by delivering projects on time with all required components. It involves meeting deadlines, adhering to specifications, and being thorough in documentation and reporting. Organizations that value completeness build reputations for reliability and quality.

In everyday life, completeness builds trust. People who follow through on commitments are often respected and relied upon. Teachers encourage completeness by assigning comprehensive evaluations and insisting on consistency and diligence in student performance.

This C reminds us that partial efforts dilute potential. In the 8C Framework, completeness elevates the standard of work and ensures that objectives are fulfilled in their entirety.

5. Conception: The Birthplace of Ideas: Conception refers to the ability to generate ideas, understand abstract concepts, and initiate new solutions. It is a domain of creativity and critical thinking. Students show strength in conception when they solve problems innovatively, think beyond the syllabus, and question the status quo.

Employees harness conception to introduce improvements, innovate services, and adapt to changing business needs. Organizations that foster a culture of conception are often industry leaders known for originality and foresight.

People in general life benefit from strong conception skills by navigating challenges with ingenuity and thinking on their feet. Teachers apply conception to design innovative teaching methods, adapt curriculum, and stimulate intellectual curiosity in students.

This component fuels transformation and progress. Within the 8C model, conception ensures that stakeholders do not merely replicate what exists but contribute fresh perspectives and solutions.

6. Cognizance: Awareness as a Superpower: Cognizance is the awareness and understanding of one's environment, capabilities, emotions, and responsibilities. For students, being cognizant involves knowing their strengths, acknowledging areas for improvement, and being mindful of academic and social contexts.

Employees need cognizance to navigate workplace dynamics, understand job roles, and maintain emotional intelligence. Organizations thrive when leadership and teams are cognizant of market conditions, internal processes, and stakeholder expectations.

People who are aware of their choices and their consequences make informed decisions. Teachers exercise cognizance by recognizing student needs, emotional states, and learning barriers. This allows for timely interventions and compassionate mentorship.

Cognizance sharpens judgment and enables responsive action. It prevents stagnation by driving informed choices and meaningful engagement across the 8C landscape.

7. Comprehensive: The Holistic View: Comprehensive thinking ensures that individuals and organizations consider all facets of a situation before making decisions. For students, this means analyzing subjects from multiple perspectives and understanding the interconnectedness of knowledge.

Employees use comprehensive thinking to address workplace challenges with full-spectrum solutions. Organizations depend on comprehensive strategies for sustainable growth, inclusive policies, and risk management In daily life, comprehensiveness supports balanced decisions and inclusive perspectives. Teachers who adopt comprehensive assessment approaches consider not just grades but also student effort, participation, and growth.

This dimension promotes thoroughness and interconnected understanding. Within the 8C Framework, comprehensive thought prevents tunnel vision and cultivates multidimensional intelligence.

8. Case Study Analysis: Learning from Real Experiences: Case Study Analysis is the art of examining real-life scenarios to extract practical insights and transferable lessons. Students engage with case studies to apply theoretical knowledge to real-world problems, enhancing understanding and critical thinking.

Employees use case studies in training and development to learn from past projects, identify best practices, and avoid recurring mistakes. Organizations analyze case studies to refine strategies and predict future outcomes.

People gain from examining life scenarios that shape decision-making, relationships, and personal growth. Teachers employ case studies to create interactive classrooms and link academic content with reality.

This component in the 8C Framework fosters experiential learning. It ensures that learning is grounded, contextual, and transformative.

The Unified Impact: Building a New Paradigm:

The 8C Framework is more than a checklist; it is a living system that integrates action, reflection, creativity, and discipline. For students, it promotes academic integrity, self-management, and career readiness. For employees, it sharpens professional capabilities, resilience, and workplace ethics. For organizations, it becomes a culture-building tool that supports excellence and adaptability.

For people in various life roles, the framework offers clarity, direction, and motivation. Teachers, who are the architects of formative years, find in the 8C Framework a robust structure for performance evaluation, mentorship, and pedagogical innovation. This holistic model nurtures potential at every level. It connects knowledge with purpose, action with awareness, and ambition with responsibility. The chapters that follow will expand each C in depth, providing real-world examples, actionable strategies, and tailored applications for each audience.

By internalizing the 8Cs, individuals and organizations can evolve into conscious contributors in a world that values not just performance but purposeful engagement. This introduction is a stepping stone toward a larger journey of excellence, one that begins with awareness and leads to impact.

****

CHAPTER – I: THE POWER OF COMMUNICATION (1C)

Building Bridges Through Expression and Understanding

Communication, in its broadest sense, is the process of transmitting information, ideas, emotions, and intentions from one person to another. This process involves much more than just speaking or writing; it encompasses the entire act of encoding and decoding messages, interpreting non-verbal cues, and ensuring that the intended message is conveyed effectively. Communication is a foundational skill for human interaction, shaping relationships, and influencing how individuals and organizations operate.

Throughout history, communication has taken many forms, evolving from simple gestures to the complex language systems we use today. From early human cave paintings to digital communication through social media platforms, the ability to communicate has shaped civilizations, driven change, and connected people across vast distances. In today's globalized world, communication has become more critical than ever, bridging cultural gaps, fostering collaboration, and enabling the flow of information in real-time.

However, despite its importance, communication is not always straightforward. It is influenced by context, culture, medium, and the dynamics between the communicators. Whether in a classroom, office, community, or at home, effective communication is the bedrock of understanding and cooperation. The challenge lies in how effectively individuals can adapt their communication style to different situations and audiences, be it students, employees, teachers, or organizations.

In the modern world, communication is not just about sharing information; it is about ensuring that the message is understood as intended, and that feedback is exchanged to refine and improve future interactions. Clear communication promotes collaboration, minimizes misunderstandings, and fosters a more harmonious and productive environment. Whether you're a student seeking clarity from a teacher, an employee negotiating a project with colleagues, or a leader guiding an organization, communication plays a central role in shaping outcomes and achieving success.

In this text, we will explore the critical role that communication plays across different audiences. By looking at the needs and challenges faced by students, employees, organizations, and teachers, we will highlight how effective communication can influence not only individual performance but also collective achievement. Understanding the various contexts in which communication occurs allows for a deeper appreciation of its impact and importance, making it easier to develop strategies to improve communication skills and foster better relationships.

1. Communication for Students: Enhancing Learning and Expression: For students, communication is a vital skill that influences not only academic success but also future career prospects. Being able to express ideas clearly, collaborate with peers, and understand complex concepts requires effective communication skills. The 8C Appraisal Framework provides a roadmap for students to assess and refine their communication skills across different scenarios.

The first step in effective communication for students is comprehension. Understanding the material being communicated — whether it is a lecture, a reading assignment, or a conversation with peers — is fundamental. In the context of the 8C Appraisal Framework, comprehension goes beyond merely hearing or reading information. It requires students to actively engage with the material, reflect on its meaning, and seek clarification when necessary. By applying comprehension effectively, students can ensure that they are not just receiving information but truly understanding it.

Context is a crucial element in communication. Students must consider the context in which the communication takes place. Whether it is a formal classroom discussion, an informal group project, or a one-on-one interaction with a professor, the context shapes how the message is delivered and received. Students need to be mindful of the context to ensure that their communication is appropriate, relevant, and effective.

Collaboration is another critical component for students to develop effective communication skills. Working with peers in group discussions, projects, or presentations requires active listening, sharing ideas, and providing constructive feedback. The 8C Appraisal Framework highlights the importance of collaboration in communication as it encourages students to work together and learn from one another. Collaborative communication fosters a learning environment that enhances both individual and group performance.

Students should also bring creativity and critical thinking into their communication. Creativity allows students to think outside the box and present information in innovative ways, while critical thinking helps them analyze and evaluate information more effectively. The 8C Appraisal Framework emphasizes the integration of creativity and critical thinking, encouraging students to engage deeply with content and communicate their ideas in meaningful and impactful ways.

For students, commitment to clear and effective communication is key to success. This commitment involves taking the time to organize thoughts, articulate ideas clearly, and ensure that the message is being understood. The 8C Appraisal Framework encourages students to be diligent and deliberate in their communication efforts, making sure that the message is both clear and concise.

2. Communication for Employees: Fostering Productivity and Teamwork: In the workplace, communication is essential for maintaining productivity, ensuring clarity, and fostering effective collaboration. Employees must be able to communicate with their colleagues, supervisors, and clients effectively to achieve both individual and organizational goals. The 8C Appraisal Framework can help employees enhance their communication skills, ensuring that they are effective in their roles and contribute to a positive work environment.

One of the primary functions of communication in the workplace is sharing information. Whether it is about project updates, meeting agendas, or company policies, employees must be able to communicate information accurately and in a timely manner. The 8C Appraisal Framework encourages employees to focus on how they share information, ensuring that it is clear, concise, and relevant to the audience.

In professional environments, the context of communication varies depending on the situation. Employees need to adapt their communication style to the context of each interaction. For example, a formal email to a client requires a different tone and structure compared to an informal conversation with a colleague. By applying the 8C Appraisal Framework, employees can assess how well they adapt their communication to different contexts, ensuring that their messages are appropriate and effective.

In many workplaces, collaboration is key to success. Employees must be able to communicate effectively within teams, sharing ideas, providing feedback, and working toward common goals. The 8C Appraisal Framework emphasizes the importance of collaboration in communication, helping employees to assess how well they work with others and communicate within team settings. Effective team communication promotes creativity, problem-solving, and overall productivity.

Critical thinking plays a significant role in workplace communication. Employees need to evaluate information, consider different perspectives, and make informed decisions. The 8C Appraisal Framework encourages employees to apply critical thinking in their communication, ensuring that they communicate decisions, suggestions, and feedback in a thoughtful and reasoned manner. By applying critical thinking, employees can contribute to more effective and strategic communication in the workplace.

Employees must demonstrate a commitment to professional communication standards, ensuring that their messages are clear, respectful, and conducive to a positive work environment. The 8C Appraisal Framework encourages employees to adhere to these standards, fostering an environment where communication is transparent, respectful, and effective.

3. Communication for Organizations: Driving Success and Innovation: For organizations, effective communication is essential for achieving business goals, fostering innovation, and building relationships with clients, employees, and other stakeholders. Communication within organizations must be clear, strategic, and aligned with the organization's objectives. The 8C Appraisal Framework provides organizations with the tools to assess and improve their communication strategies at every level, from internal communication to external messaging.

Strategic communication is critical for organizations. It involves planning how to convey messages to various stakeholders, including employees, customers, investors, and the general public. The 8C Appraisal Framework helps organizations assess their communication strategies, ensuring that they are clear, coherent, and aligned with organizational goals. A strategic approach to communication enhances organizational effectiveness and fosters long-term success.

Within an organization, communication takes place across different departments, teams, and levels of hierarchy. The 8C Appraisal Framework emphasizes the importance of understanding the context in which communication occurs. Effective communication within an organization requires an understanding of the needs and expectations of various stakeholders. By considering context, organizations can tailor their communication strategies to ensure that messages are relevant and well-received by different groups.

Collaboration is a key factor in organizational success. Organizations must foster an environment where employees collaborate effectively, share ideas, and work together toward common goals. The 8C Appraisal Framework encourages organizations to assess how well they communicate in collaborative settings, helping to identify areas for improvement and fostering a culture of teamwork

4. Communication for Personal: Personal communication is the foundation of every individual's inner and outer development. It involves the ability to express thoughts clearly, listen actively, and convey emotions with clarity and authenticity. Whether navigating relationships, setting boundaries, or articulating one's goals and needs, effective communication strengthens self-confidence and emotional intelligence. It also promotes harmony within, helping individuals align their thoughts and actions. When communication becomes intentional and reflective, it transforms everyday interactions into opportunities for deeper understanding and growth.

5. Communication for Teachers: Enhancing Student Engagement Learning: Teachers play a critical role in shaping the communication skills of their students. Effective communication in the classroom helps students understand complex concepts, engage with the material, and develop critical thinking skills. The 8C Appraisal Framework provides teachers with a structured approach to assess and improve their communication in the classroom, ensuring that they effectively engage their students.

One of the primary roles of teachers is to communicate complex ideas and concepts to students in a way that is clear and understandable. The 8C Appraisal Framework helps teachers evaluate how effectively they communicate ideas, ensuring that their messages are conveyed in a way that promotes learning and comprehension.

Effective communication in the classroom also involves creating an inclusive environment where all students feel heard, respected, and valued. Teachers must be able to communicate in a way that supports students with diverse learning needs and backgrounds. The 8C Appraisal Framework emphasizes the importance of context and collaboration in fostering an inclusive learning environment that enhances student engagement and success.

Conclusion: The Role of Communication in the 8C Appraisal Framework

In conclusion, communication is a central element of the 8C Appraisal Framework that impacts all aspects of learning, work, and personal development. By applying the principles of the framework, individuals whether students, employees, organizations, or teachers, can evaluate and improve their communication skills to enhance their success. Clear, effective communication fosters understanding, collaboration, and progress across all settings. The 8C Appraisal Framework provides a comprehensive approach to communication, helping individuals assess their ability to comprehend, contextualize, collaborate, and communicate effectively.

By prioritizing communication and applying the 8C Appraisal Framework, individuals and organizations can foster an environment where ideas are shared openly, solutions are developed collaboratively, and goals are achieved effectively.

****

CHAPTER – II: CONFIGURATION FOR SUCCESS (2C)

Structuring Thoughts, Goals, and Systems with Purpose

In today's fast-paced world, efficiency and clarity are key to success in any venture, whether it's academic, professional, or personal. The 8C Appraisal Framework, with its structured approach to organizing tasks, projects, and strategies, aims to ensure that every action, thought, and resource is effectively utilized. One of the most crucial elements in this framework is Configuration.

Configuration, in the context of 8C Appraisal Framework, refers to the foundational process of planning, structuring, and organizing every aspect of a task, project, or goal. It involves creating an effective setup that aligns resources, defines roles, and establishes clear goals, all while ensuring that every component is geared toward achieving a unified outcome. Whether for personal development, workplace tasks, or educational goals, the act of configuring properly lays the groundwork for everything that follows.

Configuration is not just about structuring tasks, it is about understanding the essence of the task or goal itself, determining the resources necessary for success, and organizing everything in a way that ensures efficiency, clarity, and achievement. It requires deep thinking, strategic planning, and the foresight to consider potential challenges, making it an indispensable element in achieving both short-term and long-term objectives.

This section will explore how Configuration can be applied to five distinct audiences: students, employees, organizations, people in general, and teachers (particularly those who assess student performance). In each case, the process of configuration plays a vital role in ensuring success, whether it's through academic planning, workplace organization, or strategic decision-making.

1. Configuration for Students: Organizing Academic Success: For students, configuring their approach to academics is crucial in ensuring that they perform well in their studies. Unlike professionals or organizations, students face the challenge of balancing multiple subjects, exams, assignments, and extracurricular activities. In this context, configuration becomes the strategy through which they organize their academic workload, set priorities, and manage their time efficiently.

At the heart of configuring their academic success is time management. Students need to allocate enough time for each subject, ensure they cover all necessary topics, and break down assignments into manageable tasks. Without proper configuration, it's easy to feel overwhelmed, especially during exam periods or when facing multiple deadlines. Configuration helps students map out a study schedule that allows them to give adequate attention to each subject while ensuring there's time for rest and rejuvenation.

Another important aspect of configuration for students is resource management. This involves identifying and organizing study materials, such as textbooks, notes, online resources, and even collaborative study sessions. Effective configuration ensures that students have all the tools they need to succeed, and they know how to access and use these resources efficiently.

Goal setting is another key component of configuration. Students need to define clear academic goals — whether it's getting a certain grade, mastering a particular subject, or improving a specific skill. Configuration helps students break down these goals into actionable steps. Setting short-term and long-term academic objectives allows students to track their progress and stay motivated throughout the semester.

In addition, configuring their learning environment plays an essential role. Students need to ensure they have a quiet, organized space conducive to focused study. Proper lighting, comfortable seating, and minimizing distractions are crucial elements in configuring a space that encourages productivity and effective learning.

Through thoughtful configuration, students are better prepared to tackle their academic challenges with confidence, clarity, and purpose.

2. Configuration for Employees: Optimizing Work Efficiency: For employees, configuration is about organizing their day-to-day activities in a way that maximizes productivity and efficiency. The workplace is often full of competing demands, tight deadlines, and a constant flow of tasks. Without proper configuration, it's easy to lose track of priorities and miss important milestones.

The first step in configuration for employees is task prioritization. Understanding which tasks are the most urgent and important helps employees stay focused on what truly matters. This involves analyzing each task's significance and urgency, creating a clear roadmap of what needs to be accomplished, and setting deadlines for each task. Prioritization ensures that employees are not only working hard but are working on the right things that drive results.

Time management is another crucial aspect of configuration for employees. Configuring their workday effectively involves allocating time for meetings, emails, project work, and breaks. Employees who fail to plan their time risk feeling overwhelmed, which can lead to burnout and decreased productivity. By setting clear work hours and ensuring that time is used efficiently, employees are able to make the most of their time at work.

Resource allocation is also a vital consideration. Employees must ensure that they have access to the necessary tools, technologies, and support to carry out their tasks efficiently. This could mean having the right software, a well-maintained computer, or access to training that can enhance their performance. Configuration ensures that these resources are available and ready for use when needed.

Another key element in configuration for employees is role definition. This is especially important in team settings, where each employee needs to clearly understand their responsibilities and how their work contributes to the team's success. Configuring roles and responsibilities ensures that everyone is on the same page and can collaborate effectively toward a common goal.

Through effective configuration, employees are able to organize their workload, manage their time, and allocate resources efficiently, leading to improved job performance and job satisfaction.

3. Configuration for Organizations: Strategic Planning for Success: At the organizational level, configuration takes on a broader scope. It involves creating a structured framework that aligns the company's goals with its available resources, personnel, and strategies. Organizational configuration is a key determinant of success because it ensures that all efforts are coordinated and directed toward achieving the company's overarching objectives.

The first step in organizational configuration is strategic alignment. Companies must align their strategies with their resources and capabilities. This involves defining clear business goals, identifying the resources needed to achieve those goals, and determining the best way to deploy those resources effectively. Configuration allows organizations to map out a clear path toward success and to remain focused on their strategic objectives.

Team structuring is another vital element of organizational configuration. By defining roles and responsibilities clearly, organizations can ensure that each team member knows their specific contribution to the company's mission. Proper configuration ensures that departments and teams are set up in such a way that there is no redundancy, and every function contributes to the overall success of the organization.

In addition, process mapping is an integral part of configuration in organizations. This refers to designing workflows that support efficient operations. By optimizing internal processes, companies can streamline their operations, reduce bottlenecks, and improve overall productivity.

Lastly, resource management is a critical aspect of configuration for organizations. Whether it's financial resources, human capital, or technology, ensuring that all resources are properly allocated and utilized is key to organizational success. Proper configuration ensures that resources are available when needed and that they are used efficiently to meet the company's objectives.

With thoughtful configuration, organizations can ensure that their strategies, resources, and teams are all aligned to achieve maximum effectiveness.

4. Configuration for People: Personal Organization and Goal Setting: When applied to individuals, configuration refers to the process of organizing their personal lives, goals, and resources to achieve success. Personal configuration is essential because it helps individuals take control of their time and resources, ensuring they are working towards their personal and professional aspirations.

For individuals, the first step in configuration is time management. Allocating time for work, leisure, and personal growth ensures that individuals can strike a balance between their responsibilities and desires. Effective time management prevents burnout and promotes a healthier work-life balance.

Goal setting is another crucial aspect of personal configuration. Individuals need to define clear, measurable goals in various aspects of their life, whether personal, professional, or financial. Configuration helps them break down these goals into actionable steps and track their progress over time. Whether it's a short-term goal like completing a project or a long-term goal like achieving career advancement, configuration ensures that there is a clear path toward success.

Resource management is also an essential component of personal configuration. This includes managing finances, skills, tools, and networks effectively. When individuals configure their resources properly, they are able to achieve more with less, ensuring that they are making the best use of what they have.

By configuring their personal goals, time, and resources, individuals can lead more fulfilling and successful lives, both personally and professionally.

5. Configuration for Teachers: Structuring the Learning Experience: Teachers are responsible for creating a learning environment that fosters growth and success for their students. Configuration in the context of teaching involves planning, structuring, and organizing lessons and assessments in a way that maximizes student engagement and learning outcomes.

The first element of configuration "for 'Teachers is lesson planning. Teachers need to create clear objectives for each lesson, ensuring that students understand the goals they are expected to achieve. Planning the lesson structure and choosing appropriate teaching methods and materials are key components of configuration. Teachers must ensure that the lesson flows logically and that activities are designed to reinforce key concepts.

Classroom management is another vital aspect of configuration. Teachers must ensure that the classroom environment is organized and conducive to learning. This includes arranging seating, providing necessary materials, and maintaining a positive, focused atmosphere. Classroom configuration supports the teacher's efforts to deliver content effectively and keep students engaged.

Finally, assessment design plays a significant role in the configuration process. Teachers must develop assessments that accurately measure student progress and understanding. This includes quizzes, exams, projects, and other forms of evaluation. Configuration ensures that assessments align with learning objectives and provide meaningful feedback that guides students toward improvement.

Through thoughtful configuration, teachers can create a structured learning environment that supports student success and fosters a positive educational experience.

Conclusion:

Configuration is a crucial element of the 8C Appraisal Framework, and its applications vary across different audiences. Whether you're a student, employee, organization, individual, or teacher, configuration helps set the stage for success by ensuring that resources are properly allocated, roles are clearly defined, and goals are systematically achieved. Proper configuration allows individuals and organizations to stay organized, focused, and aligned with their objectives, leading to enhanced performance, efficiency, and satisfaction in their respective fields.

****

CHAPTER – III: CHRONICLE OF GROWTH (3C)

Documenting Progress, Reflection, and Milestones

Chronicle, in the 8C Appraisal Framework, represents the essence of tracking, recording, and analyzing past events, actions, and decisions. It is a process of documenting and reflecting upon what has occurred to better understand how it affects the present and can influence future actions. Chronicle serves as both a record and a source of insights that help individuals, teams, and organizations refine their strategies, improve decision-making, and continuously evolve.

The concept of Chronicle is not merely about logging events; it involves interpreting the significance of these events and understanding their impact on future planning. This can be particularly useful in contexts such as goal-setting, performance analysis, and continuous improvement. By chronically tracking progress, failures, and successes, people gain a deeper understanding of patterns that emerge over time. These patterns can guide future actions, helping individuals and organizations make better decisions.

For students, employees, organizations, people in general, and teachers who assess student performance, Chronicle becomes a tool that facilitates personal growth, professional development, and educational advancement. Whether it's about monitoring academic progress, tracking professional milestones, managing organizational change, or reflecting on personal development, Chronicle plays a crucial role in maintaining clarity and direction.

This chapter will explore the application of the Chronicle concept for the aforementioned audiences, providing insights into how each can benefit from effectively documenting and analyzing their experiences.

1. Chronicle for Students: Tracking the Growth: For students, Chronicle represents a vital process of tracking their academic journey. It's more than just noting down grades or test results; it involves reflecting on learning experiences, documenting progress, and identifying areas of strength and weakness. This process not only helps students track their performance but also encourages them to become more self-aware of their academic patterns and growth trajectory.

Academic Reflection is a significant part of the Chronicle process. Students can keep journals or diaries where they reflect on each subject, the challenges they faced, and how they overcame them. By chronicling their thoughts and experiences, students can gain a deeper understanding of their learning processes, which can help them improve in future endeavors. The practice of writing about challenges, successes, and lessons learned encourages a growth mindset and a deeper connection with the subject matter.

Tracking Achievements and Setbacks also plays a crucial role. By keeping a chronological record of assignments, projects, exams, and results, students can track their academic milestones. This approach helps in visualizing their academic progress over time and enables them to celebrate small victories. Similarly, setbacks or areas where improvement is needed can be identified early, allowing for timely interventions and targeted strategies for improvement.

Goal Setting and Progress Monitoring is another essential aspect of Chronicle for students. Students can set both short-term and long-term goals and track their progress toward achieving them. With a clear chronicle of their academic journey, students can reflect on what strategies worked and what didn't, adjusting their methods for greater effectiveness. This practice encourages proactive learning and allows students to take ownership of their educational outcomes.

Through chronicling their academic experiences, students not only track their progress but also gain insights into the best ways to approach their studies, leading to more effective learning strategies and improved academic results.

2. Chronicle for Employees: Tracking Career Milestones: For employees, Chronicle serves as a tool for documenting their career journey, achievements, and professional development. Just like students, employees benefit from tracking their progress over time, whether in terms of skill acquisition, job performance, or career advancement. Chronicling career events enables employees to gain clarity on where they have been, where they are now, and where they want to go.

Career Reflection is an essential element for employees. By maintaining a detailed record of professional milestones, employees can track their growth within the organization. Whether it's reflecting on promotions, new skills learned, or challenges faced, employees who chronicle their careers can gain valuable insights into their professional strengths and areas needing development.

Performance Tracking is another significant application of Chronicle. By keeping a detailed log of key performance indicators, such as completed projects, achievements, and feedback received, employees can assess their own performance over time. This tracking process allows them to identify patterns, such as consistently high performance in specific tasks or areas that require improvement. A clear chronicle of achievements and feedback gives employees concrete evidence of their professional growth and helps them set future career goals.

Skills Development and Certifications are other important aspects to chronicle. Employees who actively document their skills, certifications, and additional training can keep track of their qualifications and professional development. This record not only aids in self-assessment but also helps in future job applications, promotions, or performance reviews. It serves as a concrete proof of their career trajectory and professional competencies.

In summary, employees who regularly chronicle their careers are better positioned to understand their professional growth, set realistic career goals, and proactively seek opportunities for advancement or improvement.

3. Chronicle for Organizations: Documenting Organizational Change: For organizations, Chronicle involves tracking the evolution of the company, its strategies, and its internal and external environments. It is a vital tool for understanding how the company has grown, adapted, and responded to changes over time. By chronicling significant events, business decisions, market trends, and organizational shifts, companies can reflect on their journey and use that insight to make informed future decisions.

Organizational History and Reflection is at the heart of Chronicle for organizations. By maintaining a detailed record of key events such as mergers, acquisitions, leadership changes, product launches, and other major decisions, companies can trace their evolution and better understand how past decisions have shaped their current position. This reflection helps organizations learn from their past and avoid repeating mistakes while building on successful strategies.

Strategic Planning and Adjustment is another critical aspect. With a chronicled record of past strategic decisions, organizations can assess their effectiveness over time. For example, by tracking the outcomes of different marketing campaigns or product launches, organizations can adjust future strategies for greater success. The Chronicle process helps companies make data-driven decisions, ensuring that future actions are based on lessons learned from the past.

Employee Development and Retention also benefits from Chronicle in organizations. By documenting the performance and development of employees over time, organizations can identify top performers, monitor career trajectories, and create personalized development plans. Tracking employee progress and development over time allows for better retention strategies and ensures that employees have the resources and support needed to thrive within the company.

In essence, Chronicle provides organizations with a framework for reflecting on their past, making informed decisions in the present, and charting a course for future growth and success.

4. Chronicle for People: Personal Reflection and Growth: For individuals, Chronicle is a tool for personal reflection, self-improvement, and life planning. By tracking life events, decisions, and experiences, people can gain a deeper understanding of their personal growth, challenges, and successes. The process of chronicle extends beyond just remembering what has happened; it's about learning from the past and using that knowledge to make better decisions moving forward.

Personal Milestones and Reflection form a significant part of Chronicle for people. Recording major life events, such as achievements, challenges, and changes, helps individuals reflect on their journey. Whether it's documenting personal successes like buying a home or overcoming a significant challenge, chronicling these moments provides a sense of accomplishment and perspective on growth.

Self-Improvement Tracking is another important aspect. By tracking personal goals such as fitness achievements, financial milestones, or learning new skills, people can monitor their self-improvement journey. Chronicle allows individuals to assess their progress in various areas of life, helping them identify what works and what needs adjustment. This process fosters a growth mindset, encouraging individuals to continuously evolve.

Life Planning and Decision Making are also critical parts of personal chronicle. When individuals document their decisions and outcomes over time, they gain valuable insights into their decision-making processes. Chronicle helps individuals understand their patterns of behaviour, the choices they've made, and how those choices have shaped their current life. This reflection can guide future decisions, helping people make more informed and intentional choices moving forward.

Through chronicling personal experiences and milestones, individuals can gain greater clarity, foster personal growth, and enhance their ability to make decisions that align with their values and long-term goals.

5. Chronicle for Teachers: Assessing Student Performance and Growth: For teachers, Chronicle serves as a crucial tool for assessing student progress, tracking academic growth, and refining teaching methods. Teachers who chronicle their students' learning journeys are able to better understand their strengths, challenges, and areas for improvement. By maintaining a detailed record of students' performance, teachers can provide more personalized and effective guidance.

Tracking Student Progress is a central element of Chronicle for teachers. By documenting each student's performance on assignments, exams, and projects, teachers can assess individual growth over time. This record helps teachers identify students who may be struggling and need additional support, as well as those who are excelling and may benefit from advanced challenges.

Reflection on Teaching Methods is another important aspect. Teachers who chronicle their teaching methods, lesson plans, and outcomes can assess what strategies were effective and which ones need improvement. This process helps educators refine their teaching approaches, making adjustments to ensure that all students have the best chance of success.

Providing Constructive Feedback is facilitated by chronicling student performance. Teachers who maintain a record of their students' progress are better able to provide specific, actionable feedback. By looking back at students past performance, teachers can offer guidance that is tailored to individual needs and challenges, helping students improve and reach their academic goals.

For teachers, Chronicle is not just about tracking student performance; it's a reflective practice that helps improve both teaching effectiveness and student outcomes.

Conclusion:

Chronicle, as part of the 8C Appraisal Framework, offers immense value across various audiences. Whether it's for students tracking academic progress, employees monitoring career growth, organizations assessing strategic success, individuals reflecting on personal development, or teachers evaluating student performance, the power of documenting and reflecting on past experiences cannot be underestimated. By chronicling their journeys, all these groups can gain insights into their progress, make informed decisions, and continue to evolve in a structured and intentional way.

The concept of Chronicle is universal, and its application can lead to meaningful improvements in personal, academic, and professional contexts. Through the act of chronicling, individuals and organizations alike can gain clarity, learn from the past, and build a more informed and prosperous future.

****

CHAPTER – IV: COMPLETENESS AS A STAND(4C)

Delivering With Accuracy, Integrity, and Responsibility

Completeness in the 8C Appraisal Framework refers to the thoroughness and wholeness with which tasks, goals, or assessments are executed. It signifies that all aspects of an objective, task, or assessment process are fulfilled, leaving no part unaddressed. In an appraisal context, completeness is essential to ensure that every part of the evaluation process is covered, and no critical elements are overlooked.

When applied to academic, professional, and organizational settings, completeness helps in building a holistic view of performance. It ensures that all relevant factors are considered and that any gaps in understanding or execution are identified. For students, completeness means ensuring that all aspects of a subject are studied, for employees, it means covering all tasks in their job roles. For organizations, it refers to comprehensive evaluations of processes and strategies. For individuals and teachers, completeness ensures that goals and assessments are fully met, and no aspect is left behind.

In the context of the 8C Appraisal Framework, completeness helps guide individuals, teams, and organizations toward a more rounded and inclusive approach to evaluation. It promotes thoroughness in understanding, execution, and reflection, leading to better outcomes and more meaningful assessments. This concept plays a vital role in ensuring that all relevant data points, achievements, and challenges are considered before final decisions are made.

The following sections will explore how the concept of completeness can be applied to students, employees, organizations, people, and teachers, offering insights into how each can benefit from adopting this principle in their appraisal processes.

1. Completeness for Students: Comprehensive Academic Evaluation: For students, completeness involves ensuring that every aspect of their academic journey is covered, from mastering core concepts to participating in all assignments, tests, and projects. Academic evaluations often miss critical dimensions if students are not thorough in their approach to learning. Completeness here ensures that students don't leave any gaps in their knowledge or skills.

Holistic Learning is central to the concept of completeness for students. It is about ensuring that all subjects or topics within a course are studied with equal focus. By addressing every aspect of the curriculum, students ensure that they are not only prepared for exams but also gain a deeper understanding of each subject area. Completeness encourages students to study comprehensively, explore topics beyond the prescribed syllabus, and fill in gaps that might hinder overall performance.

Active Participation in Assessments also forms a part of completeness for students. It's not enough to simply attend classes or read textbooks; students must engage in all forms of assessments; whether quizzes, assignments, presentations, or group projects. By ensuring active involvement in every assessment, students can ensure that their abilities are tested in multiple contexts, reflecting a complete understanding of the material.

Self-Reflection and Feedback Integration are critical components of completeness for students. This involves taking into account not just grades but also feedback from instructors, peers, and self-assessments. A complete academic evaluation comes from addressing areas of improvement highlighted in feedback and actively working on those aspects to ensure holistic development. By considering feedback as part of their learning journey, students can track their growth over time and make adjustments to their study methods as needed.

Completeness in the academic context helps students become well-rounded learners, enhancing their capacity for critical thinking, problem-solving, and adaptability. It pushes students to consider all aspects of their educational experience, ensuring no area is overlooked.

2. Completeness for Employees: Comprehensive Job Performance: For employees, completeness means thoroughly fulfilling all aspects of their job roles, ensuring that no part of their responsibilities is neglected. In a professional setting, job performance is not just about completing tasks but about meeting all objectives and expectations in a thorough, detailed manner.

Task Fulfillment is one of the key elements of completeness for employees. Employees need to ensure that every task assigned is fully completed, and every expectation set by their managers or teams is met. A complete job performance evaluation considers not only the quality but also the quantity and timeliness of task completion. By fulfilling every assigned responsibility in detail, employees demonstrate their reliability and commitment.

Skill Development and Versatility is another crucial component of completeness. Employees should work on developing a broad skill set that aligns with their roles and the company's goals. This includes enhancing both technical and soft skills. A complete employee evaluation takes into account the breadth of skills that an individual has developed, not just their proficiency in specific tasks. Employees who actively seek to develop a wide range of skills are often valued for their ability to adapt to changing job demands.

Meeting Organizational Goals and KPIs also highlights the importance of completeness. An employee's job performance is not just evaluated based on their individual tasks but also on how well they contribute to broader organizational goals. A complete employee evaluation looks at how well an individual's contributions support the strategic objectives of the organization, ensuring that they are aligned with the company's mission and vision.

When employees focus on completeness, they demonstrate their commitment to personal growth, excellence, and the broader success of the organization. By taking a comprehensive approach to their roles, employees can position themselves for career advancement, better performance reviews, and increased job satisfaction.

3. Completeness for Organizations: Comprehensive Performance and Strategy Evaluation: In an organizational context, completeness refers to thoroughly assessing every aspect of the business — whether it's performance, strategy, operations, or employee engagement. Organizations need to evaluate not just individual metrics but the complete picture of their business, ensuring they address both successes and areas for improvement.

Strategic Goals and Alignment are central to the completeness of an organization. For a business to be truly effective, every part of the organization must be working toward common strategic goals. Completeness involves aligning all departments, teams, and resources with the overarching goals of the organization. This alignment ensures that there are no conflicting priorities and that all efforts are directed toward common objectives.

Comprehensive Process Review is another crucial aspect of completeness for organizations. Organizations need to review every process — whether related to production, customer service, or internal operations. A complete organizational evaluation involves identifying inefficiencies, gaps, or potential areas for innovation. By addressing every aspect of their operations, organizations can streamline processes and improve overall efficiency.

Employee Engagement and Performance also form an essential part of organizational completeness. Organizations must evaluate not only the financial performance but also the engagement levels and performance of their employees. Regular performance appraisals, feedback loops, and engagement surveys help organizations assess the overall satisfaction and effectiveness of their workforce. A complete organizational evaluation considers both tangible and intangible factors, ensuring that all aspects of business performance are addressed.

By embracing completeness in their evaluations, organizations can develop more effective strategies, optimize operations, and improve employee morale. This holistic approach ensures that no aspect of the organization's performance is overlooked.

4. Completeness for People: Comprehensive Personal Growth and Reflection:
For individuals, completeness means a holistic approach to self-improvement, ensuring that every area of personal development is addressed. It involves reflecting on one's goals, actions, and outcomes to ensure that there are no areas of life left unexamined or underdeveloped.

Self-Reflection and Awareness is a key element of completeness for individuals. Personal growth is about understanding who you are, your strengths, weaknesses, and areas of opportunity. By reflecting on experiences, decisions, and actions, individuals can ensure they are addressing all aspects of their personal development. This reflection process helps individuals grow emotionally, intellectually, and spiritually, contributing to a well-rounded life.

Goal Setting and Achievement is another important aspect of completeness. People need to set clear, achievable goals in all areas of their lives—whether related to health, career, relationships, or personal interests. Completeness ensures that individuals evaluate their goals regularly, assess progress, and make adjustments as needed. By setting comprehensive goals and tracking progress in all areas, individuals can achieve a balanced life that addresses all their needs.

Learning and Adaptability also contribute to personal completeness. It's essential for individuals to continue learning and adapting throughout their lives. Whether through formal education, personal hobbies, or life experiences, individuals should aim to acquire new skills, broaden their knowledge, and grow in various aspects of life. Completeness in this context means actively seeking opportunities to learn and improve, making adjustments along the way.

Completeness for individuals is about becoming the best version of oneself by addressing all areas of life and striving for continuous growth and development. It encourages people to take a holistic approach to their personal journey, leading to greater fulfillment and success.

5. Completeness for Teachers: Comprehensive Student Evaluation: For teachers, completeness means ensuring that all aspects of a student's learning and progress are fully evaluated. It involves assessing not only the academic performance but also the personal and behavioral growth of students. A complete evaluation helps teachers identify areas of strength and weakness in their students and provides a foundation for offering meaningful feedback and guidance.

Holistic Student Assessment is a central element of completeness for teachers. Teachers should evaluate students in a comprehensive manner, considering not just test scores but also factors such as effort, participation, and improvement over time. By assessing all aspects of student performance, teachers can provide more personalized and meaningful feedback, helping students understand their strengths and areas for development.

Feedback and Support are essential components of completeness for teachers. A complete evaluation process includes providing students with timely, constructive feedback that helps them improve. Teachers should ensure that their assessments are thorough, offering suggestions for improvement and recognizing accomplishments. This type of feedback motivates students to continue learning and refining their skills.

Progress Tracking and Goal Setting are also important for completeness in student evaluation. Teachers need to track students' progress throughout the year and set goals for future improvement. A complete assessment system ensures that students are not only evaluated based on their final outcomes but are also given a chance to improve and grow over time.

By applying the concept of completeness in assessments, teachers can provide a more thorough, fair, and balanced evaluation of their students, helping them reach their full potential.

Conclusion:

Completeness in the 8C Appraisal Framework is a transformative principle that drives thorough evaluation and reflection across different audiences. Whether it is students ensuring they grasp all subjects, employees fulfilling their job roles comprehensively, organizations evaluating their entire performance, individuals working on self-improvement, or teachers assessing all aspects of student growth, the value of completeness cannot be overstated.

Incorporating completeness into the appraisal process leads to more effective decision-making, clearer understanding, and enhanced growth for individuals, teams, and organizations. It encourages the examination of all facets of performance, ensuring that no aspect is left behind, and supports continuous improvement across various domains.

As organizations, educators, and individuals adopt the principle of completeness, they ensure that progress is holistic, well-rounded, and deeply reflective, paving the way for a future built on thoughtful evaluation and comprehensive development.

****

CHAPTER – V: COGNIZANCE IN ACTION (5C)

Cultivating Awareness for Personal and Social Intelligence

Cognizance, in the context of the 8C Appraisal Framework, refers to the level of awareness, attention, and understanding that individuals or organizations possess regarding their roles, responsibilities, strengths, weaknesses, and the broader environment in which they operate. It is an essential component of the appraisal process as it enables effective decision-making, self-awareness, and action. Cognizance involves more than just awareness; it extends to a deeper comprehension of one's surroundings and how they influence actions and outcomes.

In the process of appraising performance or assessing progress, cognizance is vital. It ensures that individuals and organizations are fully aware of the context in which they operate, the factors influencing their actions, and the potential outcomes of their decisions. By fostering cognizance, the 8C Appraisal Framework encourages a reflective approach that not only highlights what has been accomplished but also considers how the environment, challenges, and personal perceptions shape actions.

The application of cognizance goes beyond mere recognition of factors. It involves developing a deeper understanding of complex dynamics, enabling individuals and groups to make informed choices. This awareness extends to understanding one's own abilities and limitations, the expectations of others, and the broader societal, organizational, and professional context.

In the following sections, we will explore how the concept of cognizance can be applied to students, employees, organizations, people, and teachers. We will look at how each group can benefit from cultivating awareness and how cognizance influences their development, performance, and success in their respective fields.

1. Cognizance for Students: Developing Awareness of Learning and Growth:
For students, cognizance is central to academic success and personal development. It involves not only understanding the subjects being studied but also being aware of the external factors that influence their learning, such as time management, study habits, and the learning environment. By cultivating cognizance, students can develop a deeper understanding of their strengths and weaknesses, as well as the areas where improvement is needed.

Self-Assessment and Reflection form the foundation of cognizance for students. By regularly reflecting on their academic performance, students can evaluate their progress and identify areas that require more focus. This self-awareness allows them to adjust their learning strategies to better align with their strengths. When students are cognizant of their own learning process, they are better equipped to tackle challenges and capitalize on opportunities for improvement.

Awareness of External Influences is another critical aspect of cognizance for students. A student's academic journey is influenced by various external factors, including family, social life, and extracurricular activities. By acknowledging and understanding these influences, students can manage their time and energy more effectively, ensuring a balanced approach to learning. Cognizance allows students to recognize when these external factors may be detracting from their focus and take proactive steps to mitigate distractions.

Engagement with Learning Opportunities is also a part of being cognizant as a student. This means being aware of the various resources available to support academic success, such as tutoring services, academic counselling, and extracurricular activities. Students who actively seek out and engage with these opportunities are better equipped to succeed academically and personally.

Cognizance allows students to develop a more holistic view of their education, giving them the tools they need to make informed decisions and achieve their academic and personal goals.

2. **Cognizance for Employees: Awareness of Job Roles and Organizational Goals:** For employees, cognizance involves a comprehensive understanding of their job roles, the organization's goals, and how their performance contributes to the overall success of the company. By developing cognizance, employees can improve their productivity, enhance their personal growth, and align their efforts with the organization's objectives.

Understanding Job Expectations is the first step for employees in cultivating cognizance. Employees must be fully aware of their job responsibilities, the skills required, and the expected outcomes. This awareness allows them to perform their tasks effectively and ensures they are meeting or exceeding expectations. Employees who are cognizant of their role are more likely to take ownership of their tasks and deliver high-quality work.

Alignment with Organizational Goals is another key aspect of cognizance for employees. An employee who understands the organization's mission, vision, and strategic goals can align their individual objectives with the company's overarching goals. This alignment creates a sense of purpose and motivation, as employees can see how their contributions fit into the larger picture. Cognizant employees are better able to prioritize tasks that directly impact the organization's success, contributing to its growth and development.

Awareness of Professional Development Opportunities is also crucial for employees. Cognizance encourages employees to be proactive in identifying opportunities for career advancement, skill development, and personal growth. By recognizing the skills and competencies needed for future roles, employees can take steps to acquire them, positioning themselves for career advancement.

Cognizance in the workplace leads to greater job satisfaction, improved performance, and a more engaged workforce. When employees are aware of their roles, goals, and opportunities, they are better equipped to make meaningful contributions to their organization.

3. Cognizance for Organizations: Understanding Internal and External Factors:

For organizations, cognizance involves a deep understanding of both internal and external factors that impact the business's performance. It means being aware of market trends, consumer behaviour, technological advancements, and the competitive landscape. Internally, it includes understanding employee needs, organizational culture, and the effectiveness of business operations.

Market Awareness and Adaptation is a key element of organizational cognizance. Organizations must stay informed about changes in the market, such as shifts in consumer preferences, emerging technologies, and new regulations. By cultivating cognizance of these external factors, organizations can adapt their strategies, products, and services to stay competitive. A business that is aware of market trends is better positioned to innovate and meet the evolving needs of its customers.

Internal Awareness of Operations and Culture is equally important. Organizations must have a clear understanding of their internal processes, workflows, and organizational culture. Cognizance in this context involves assessing the strengths and weaknesses of business operations, identifying areas for improvement, and fostering a culture of collaboration and transparency. An organization that is aware of its internal dynamics can optimize its processes, improve employee engagement, and create a more efficient and productive work environment.

Employee Engagement and Well-Being is another critical factor for organizational cognizance. Organizations must be aware of their employees' needs, aspirations, and challenges. This awareness enables organizations to create a supportive environment where employees feel valued and motivated. By regularly engaging with employees and seeking feedback, organizations can address issues before they become significant problems and create a work environment conducive to productivity and innovation.

Cognizance in organizations is the foundation for strategic decision-making, innovation, and long-term success. By being aware of both internal and external factors, organizations can make informed choices that lead to growth and sustainability.

4. **Cognizance for People: Self-Awareness and Personal Development:** For individuals, cognizance is a critical tool for personal development and achieving life goals. It involves understanding one's strengths, weaknesses, values, and goals. Cognizant individuals are more self-aware and are better equipped to navigate the challenges they face in their personal and professional lives.

Self-Reflection and Personal Growth are integral to personal cognizance. Individuals must regularly assess their actions, behaviors, and decisions to understand how they align with their values and aspirations. This process of self-reflection helps people identify areas for growth and improvement, enabling them to make better choices in the future. A cognizant individual is aware of their emotional triggers, decision-making patterns, and behaviours, which allows for more effective self-regulation and personal growth.

Understanding Relationships and Social Dynamics is another important aspect of personal cognizance. Individuals who are aware of their interactions with others and the impact of their behaviours on relationships are better equipped to build strong, healthy connections. Cognizance of social dynamics enables individuals to navigate challenging social situations, communicate effectively, and foster positive relationships in both personal and professional settings.

Awareness of Life's Opportunities and Challenges is equally important. Cognizant individuals are mindful of the opportunities and challenges that come their way. They are proactive in seeking opportunities for growth, whether through new experiences, education, or career advancements. At the same time, they are aware of the challenges they may face and are prepared to confront them with resilience and determination.

Cognizance empowers individuals to lead fulfilling lives by making informed decisions, building strong relationships, and embracing opportunities for growth.

5. Cognizance for Teachers: Holistic Student Assessment and Development: For teachers, cognizance involves a comprehensive understanding of their students' needs, strengths, and weaknesses. It also means being aware of the broader educational environment, including curriculum requirements, student behaviour, and external influences that affect student performance.

Understanding Students' Needs is essential for teachers who aim to provide personalized and effective instruction. By being aware of the unique needs of each student, teachers can adapt their teaching methods and materials to ensure that all students have the opportunity to succeed. Cognizance allows teachers to recognize when a student is struggling or excelling and to adjust their approach accordingly.

Awareness of Educational Environment also plays a critical role in teaching. Teachers must be cognizant of the broader context in which they teach, including societal trends, technological advancements, and changes in educational policies. This awareness allows teachers to incorporate relevant content and teaching methods into their lessons, ensuring that students are equipped for the challenges they will face in the real world.

Effective Student Assessment is another area where cognizance is key. Teachers who are aware of the full spectrum of student performance, including emotional, social, and academic factors, can provide more accurate and comprehensive assessments. This holistic approach ensures that assessments reflect the overall development of the student, not just their academic achievements.

Cognizance in teaching leads to a more inclusive, effective, and compassionate learning environment. Teachers who develop cognizance of their students' needs and the broader educational context can foster a supportive and motivating atmosphere that encourages student growth and success.

Conclusion:

Cognizance, as a critical component of the 8C Appraisal Framework, plays a significant role in shaping the effectiveness of performance assessments across various domains. Whether it is students gaining self-awareness of their learning process, employees aligning their efforts with organizational goals, organizations adapting to market trends, individuals improving their personal growth, or teachers offering comprehensive assessments, cognizance is at the heart of informed decision-making and continuous improvement. By cultivating cognizance, individuals and organizations can make better decisions, improve their performance, and foster growth. It is through awareness and understanding of one's own capabilities and external influences that we can achieve our fullest potential and contribute meaningfully to our environments. The application of cognizance leads to a more reflective, adaptive, and successful approach to personal and professional development.

****

CHAPTER – VI: CONCEPTION OF IDEAS (6C)

Sparking Innovation Through Creative Thinking

Conception, as part of the 8C Appraisal Framework, plays an essential role in shaping how individuals and organizations view their roles, goals, and opportunities. At its core, conception refers to the way in which a person or entity forms ideas, constructs visions, and interprets experiences to guide actions and decisions. It is the mental process by which we understand our surroundings, identify problems, and create solutions. Within an appraisal framework, conception becomes a powerful tool for guiding growth, defining success, and shaping behaviours.

In essence, conception is about how individuals or organizations mentally structure their goals, strategies, and understanding of the world. It involves perception, reasoning, and the formulation of plans that align with one's values and objectives. In an appraisal setting, this mental process is key to understanding performance, measuring success, and setting new targets. By honing their conception skills, individuals and organizations can clarify their direction, assess their past actions more effectively, and plan for a successful future.

The 8C Appraisal Framework provides a structure for assessing performance and development. Conception, as one of its core components, plays a significant role in this framework by helping individuals and organizations conceptualize their strategies and goals. Conception goes beyond simple goal-setting. It is about creating a clear vision and a structured approach to achieving that vision, whether in personal development, workplace performance, or organizational strategy. This exploration will look at how conception impacts five distinct groups: students, employees, organizations, people, and teachers. Each of these groups can leverage the power of conception to foster growth, achieve success, and continually refine their approach to performance and progress.

1. **Conception for Students: Shaping Academic Goals and Learning Strategies:** For students, conception is crucial in determining how they approach their education and academic goals. The way students conceptualize their learning process can significantly influence their academic performance and long-term success.

Defining Educational Goals is the starting point for students in shaping their academic conception. Conception helps students define their vision for their education. By understanding the bigger picture and setting clear, achievable goals, students are better equipped to direct their efforts and prioritize their studies. Whether it's aiming for a specific grade, mastering a subject, or preparing for a future career, how a student conceives their academic journey sets the tone for their approach to learning.

Strategizing for Success is another key area where conception plays a vital role. Students need to create strategies for managing their time, understanding their subjects, and navigating challenges in the learning process. Those who have a well-formed conception of their academic journey will understand the best methods for tackling their coursework, whether it involves regular studying, seeking help from tutors, or leveraging online resources. A student who has a clear mental framework of their study approach is more likely to remain organized, focused, and on track to achieve their goals.

Overcoming Challenges requires the ability to reshape one's conception in response to obstacles. When faced with difficulties, students must reassess their approach and be flexible in their problem-solving. This can mean revising their study methods, adjusting their schedule, or developing resilience in the face of academic stress. Students who have a well-formed conception of their strengths and weaknesses are better equipped to make these adjustments and continue progressing toward their educational objectives.

Self-Reflection and Personal Growth are vital elements of student success. By regularly reflecting on their performance and conceptualizing ways to improve, students become more self-aware and can continue refining their approach to learning. This continuous process of conceptualizing improvements leads to personal growth and a more rewarding educational experience.

Conception is the foundation upon which students build their learning strategies, overcome challenges, and set themselves up for future success.

2. Conception for Employees: Understanding Job Roles and Career Paths: In the professional world, conception is an essential tool for employees in shaping their careers, understanding their roles, and aligning their personal goals with organizational objectives. A clear mental conception of one's job responsibilities, career trajectory, and workplace environment helps employees perform better and achieve their goals.

Role Clarity and Performance are among the first aspects employees need to consider when applying conception to their careers. A clear understanding of their role within the organization, the expectations tied to that role, and how their work contributes to the overall success of the business is vital. Employees who have a well-defined conception of their job responsibilities can approach their tasks with greater clarity and efficiency, leading to improved performance and job satisfaction.

Career Development and Advancement are key to employees' long-term success. Having a mental framework for their career path allows employees to take charge of their professional growth. Conception helps employees to visualize their future, set career goals, and develop skills that will move them closer to their desired position within the company or industry. By setting milestones and continuously refining their approach, employees can ensure they are on track to achieve their career ambitions.

Navigating Workplace Dynamics requires employees to conceptualize their relationships with colleagues, supervisors, and clients. Understanding the interpersonal dynamics within a workplace allows employees to develop better communication strategies, work more effectively in teams, and contribute to a positive workplace culture. Conception of workplace interactions, company culture, and team dynamics helps employees adapt to challenges and foster better collaboration.

Adapting to Change is a critical aspect of any modern work environment. Employees who have a flexible and adaptable mental framework are better positioned to navigate the challenges posed by technological advancements, changes in leadership, and shifts in business priorities. By maintaining a well-rounded conception of their role and the industry, employees can thrive in an ever-changing work environment.

For employees, conception is central to shaping their professional journey, aligning their personal and organizational goals, and continuously evolving within their careers.

3. **Conception for Organizations: Defining Strategy and Achieving Organizational Goals:** At the organizational level, conception is about defining the company's vision, strategy, and approach to growth. Organizations that cultivate a clear conception of their market, culture, and internal processes are better equipped to navigate challenges and drive success.

Strategic Vision and Mission are essential components of organizational conception. An organization must clearly define its mission and long-term vision, which guide decision-making, set priorities, and align resources. Conception at the organizational level helps executives and leaders formulate strategies that drive business growth and operational success. A strong conception of the company's core values and long-term objectives ensures that the organization remains focused on its goals and stays on course, even in the face of challenges.

Innovation and Market Awareness also play a central role in organizational conception. In a rapidly evolving market, organizations must continuously assess their surroundings and develop new products, services, and strategies. A well-formed conception of market trends, consumer behaviour, and emerging technologies helps organizations stay ahead of the curve and maintain their competitive edge. Conception here is about understanding the ever-changing landscape and positioning the organization for future success.

Organizational Culture and Employee Engagement are integral to an organization's conception. Leaders need to have a clear understanding of their company's culture, employee needs, and the overall work environment. Conception at this level involves creating a supportive, inclusive, and productive culture that motivates employees and drives performance. By developing a strong internal conception, organizations can improve employee satisfaction, reduce turnover, and enhance overall performance.

Adapting to Change and Resilience are also critical aspects of organizational conception. In times of economic downturns, technological disruption, or internal restructuring, organizations with a flexible conception of their processes and goals are better positioned to adapt. By regularly revising their strategies and operations, organizations can remain resilient and maintain progress toward their long-term goals.

Conception at the organizational level is vital for ensuring that a company has a clear vision, a strategic plan, and a culture that drives success.

4. Conception for People: Personal Awareness and Development: For individuals, conception plays a fundamental role in shaping their personal development, relationships, and life goals. The way people conceive their personal values, objectives, and the challenges they face can significantly affect their overall life satisfaction and success.

Personal Identity and Self-Understanding are essential components of personal conception. Individuals must have a clear understanding of who they are, what they value, and what they hope to achieve in life. By conceptualizing their identity, people can make better decisions, choose appropriate career paths, and develop meaningful relationships. Conception helps people understand their strengths and weaknesses, fostering self-awareness and growth.

Setting and Achieving Personal Goals requires a clear conception of one's objectives. Whether it's pursuing a career, starting a family, or improving physical health, individuals need to develop a clear vision for their personal future. Conception helps people break down large, daunting goals into manageable steps, making the process of achievement more attainable and less overwhelming.

Understanding Relationships and Social Roles is also key for personal development. People's conceptions of their roles within families, communities, and social circles influence their interactions and relationships. By having a clear understanding of their roles, individuals can improve their communication, resolve conflicts, and build stronger, more fulfilling relationships with others.

Navigating Life's Challenges is a constant process that requires the ability to adapt and grow. Conception allows individuals to develop a flexible mindset and approach life's difficulties with resilience. Those who can effectively conceptualize problems and solutions are better able to navigate adversity and emerge stronger from challenges.

Cognizance of one's personal identity, goals, and relationships helps individuals cultivate a fulfilling life path, ensuring growth and well-being.

5. Conception for Teachers: Guiding Student Development and Assessment: For teachers, conception is an essential aspect of guiding students' development and assessing their academic performance. Teachers' understanding of their students' abilities, challenges, and potential is crucial for fostering an environment of growth and success.

Student Needs and Differentiation are central to teaching. Teachers must conceive each student's unique needs, learning styles, and challenges to provide personalized instruction that meets them where they are. By understanding their students' academic and emotional needs, teachers can create more effective lesson plans and provide targeted support.

Assessment and Feedback are also areas where conception plays a vital role. Teachers need to conceptualize not only the content they are teaching but also the various ways in which students engage with and internalize that content. By developing clear, fair, and comprehensive assessments, teachers can measure students' progress and provide constructive feedback that helps them improve.

Classroom Environment and Student Motivation are closely tied to teachers' conception of their students' potential. Teachers who can conceptualize an environment that is engaging, supportive, and stimulating will foster greater student participation, enthusiasm, and success. Motivating students to reach their full potential requires a deep understanding of their individual and collective needs.

Fostering Critical Thinking and Problem-Solving is a key goal for teachers. Conception helps teachers understand how students think and approach problems, allowing them to create lessons that encourage deeper engagement and higher-order thinking skills. Teachers who can conceptualize students' learning processes are more effective at guiding them toward independent thought and creative solutions.

In the classroom, conception enables teachers to guide, assess, and foster student development, ensuring that each student's unique abilities and potential are nurtured.

Conclusion:

Conception, as a central component of the 8C Appraisal Framework, serves as the guiding force behind how individuals, organizations, and educators approach growth, assessment, and development. Whether students are conceptualizing their academic journey, employees are envisioning their career paths, organizations are defining their strategies, individuals are planning their personal futures, or teachers are shaping their students' learning experiences, conception is the mental foundation that shapes decisions, drives performance, and fosters success.

By cultivating a clear and comprehensive conception in each of these domains, individuals and organizations can better navigate challenges, achieve goals, and realize their potential. In the 8C Appraisal Framework, conception empowers growth and continuous improvement by providing a structured, thoughtful approach to defining success and measuring progress. Through an understanding of conception, people are equipped to build more meaningful lives, careers, and organizations.

****

CHAPTER – VII: THE ART OF BEGINNING COMPREHENSION (7C)

Seeing the Bigger Picture with Depth and Inclusion

In the world of personal and organizational growth, comprehension holds a key role in determining how effectively individuals and entities can process, understand, and apply the information at their disposal. Comprehension, in the context of the 8C Appraisal Framework, refers to the ability to grasp concepts, interpret data, understand relationships, and make informed decisions based on that understanding. This mental capacity is central to learning, problem-solving, and achieving goals across various domains.

At its core, comprehension is about more than just reading or listening. It involves interpreting the deeper meaning behind words, actions, and scenarios. The ability to comprehend is tied to critical thinking, reflection, and application. Whether an individual is a student trying to absorb complex academic material, an employee working through professional tasks, or an organization striving to understand market trends, comprehension forms the foundation of progress.

Within the framework, comprehension plays an integral part in shaping the way goals are set, strategies are formulated, and actions are taken. For students, it influences how they grasp knowledge and apply it in exams and real-life situations. For employees, it determines how well they understand job roles, company culture, and tasks. Organizations rely on comprehension to evaluate business performance, understand customer needs, and adapt to changes.

Similarly, teachers use comprehension to assess student progress and determine areas for improvement.

The 8C Appraisal Framework emphasizes comprehension because it is fundamental to the process of personal and professional development. It ensures that individuals and groups understand not just the surface level but also the underlying principles, connections, and implications of the information they encounter. In this text, we will explore how comprehension, as part of this framework, influences five distinct groups: students, employees, organizations, people, and teachers.

1. Comprehension for Students: Mastering Learning and Academic Challenges: For students, comprehension is at the heart of academic success. The ability to understand and internalize information is the first step toward academic achievement. Comprehension enables students to grasp complex concepts, solve problems, and apply their knowledge in practical scenarios. Without strong comprehension skills, learning becomes fragmented, and academic progress is hindered.

Grasping Core Concepts is the foundation of any educational journey. For students, comprehension means being able to break down the essential elements of a subject and understand how they interconnect. Whether it's mathematics, history, or science, understanding core concepts is crucial for moving forward with more advanced topics. A student who fully comprehends the basics is better prepared to tackle higher-level challenges.

Critical Thinking and Problem Solving rely heavily on comprehension. Students who can comprehend a subject deeply are more likely to engage in critical thinking, evaluate different perspectives, and solve problems efficiently. In this context, comprehension goes beyond memorization. It is about understanding the logic and reasoning behind a problem and applying that understanding to find solutions.

Application of Knowledge is another important aspect of comprehension for students. It's not enough to simply understand a subject in theory; students must also be able to apply what they have learned in real-world scenarios. Whether in exams, projects, or practical situations, students need to be able to take their comprehension and put it into action. This ability to apply knowledge is a direct result of strong comprehension skills.

Self-Assessment and Continuous Improvement are vital for student growth. Comprehension allows students to assess their own learning and identify areas where they need further improvement. Through comprehension, students can reflect on their strengths and weaknesses, evaluate their progress, and set goals for continuous learning.

For students, strong comprehension skills form the backbone of their academic journey. They enable students to learn effectively, think critically, and apply their knowledge in meaningful ways.

2. Comprehension for Employees: Enhancing Work Performance and Career Development: In the workplace, comprehension is equally essential for career success. Employees who comprehend their tasks, job roles, and company goals are better equipped to contribute meaningfully to their organization. Strong comprehension allows employees to understand the broader business context, recognize how their work fits into the organization's mission, and make informed decisions that impact performance.

Understanding Job Roles and Expectations is the first step for employees to perform well in their roles. Comprehension allows employees to clearly understand what is expected of them and how they can best meet those expectations. Whether it's meeting deadlines, fulfilling responsibilities, or working within a team, comprehension helps employees stay aligned with organizational goals.

Navigating Complex Tasks and Projects requires a deep level of understanding. Many jobs require employees to solve complex problems or manage intricate projects. Comprehension allows employees to break down complex tasks into manageable steps and understand the resources and strategies needed to complete them successfully. Whether it's analyzing data, coordinating with colleagues, or designing solutions, comprehension ensures that employees can approach challenges with clarity and confidence.

Interpersonal Skills and Communication also benefit from strong comprehension. Employees need to understand the perspectives of their colleagues, clients, and supervisors. By comprehending the needs, motivations, and behaviors of others, employees can communicate more effectively, build better relationships, and collaborate more efficiently. This understanding improves teamwork and helps create a positive work environment.

Career Advancement and Skill Development are directly linked to comprehension. Employees who understand their strengths and areas for improvement are better positioned to take on new challenges and grow within their careers. Comprehension helps employees identify gaps in their knowledge or skills and take proactive steps to address them. Whether it's pursuing further training or seeking mentorship, employees who comprehend their developmental needs are more likely to advance in their careers.

Comprehension, in the workplace, is about more than just performing tasks. It enables employees to make better decisions, communicate effectively, and position themselves for long-term success.

3. Comprehension for Organizations: Understanding Markets and Shaping Strategy: For organizations, comprehension is a critical factor in developing effective strategies and maintaining competitive advantage. Organizations that can comprehend market trends, consumer needs, and industry developments are better positioned to make strategic decisions that drive growth and success. It enables them to understand their place within the larger industry landscape and navigate the challenges they face.

Market Research and Analysis are areas where comprehension is essential. Organizations need to comprehend market trends, customer preferences, and emerging opportunities to stay ahead of the competition. Comprehension of data, customer behaviour, and market dynamics allows organizations to make informed decisions about product development, marketing strategies, and business operations. Without this comprehension, organizations risk falling behind in an increasingly competitive marketplace.

Strategic Planning and Goal Setting require a clear understanding of the organization's current position and future prospects. Leaders must comprehend the internal and external factors that affect the organization's performance, including strengths, weaknesses, opportunities, and threats. This comprehensive understanding helps executives set realistic goals, create strategic plans, and allocate resources effectively.

Employee Engagement and Leadership Development also benefit from comprehension. Leaders need to comprehend the capabilities and aspirations of their employees to effectively manage teams and foster a positive workplace culture. By understanding their team's needs and motivations, leaders can create an environment that supports growth, innovation, and collaboration. This comprehension improves employee satisfaction and reduces turnover.

Adapting to Change and Innovation is an ongoing process for any organization. In today's fast-paced business world, organizations must comprehend technological advancements, regulatory changes, and global trends to remain adaptable. A deep understanding of these factors allows organizations to pivot when necessary and continue to evolve in response to new challenges.

For organizations, comprehension enables the development of effective strategies, improves decision-making, and ensures that the business remains competitive in an ever-changing market.

4. Comprehension for People: Personal Growth and Navigating Life's Challenges: For individuals, comprehension plays a fundamental role in personal development. The ability to understand one's environment, relationships, goals, and challenges is key to navigating life successfully. Comprehension helps people make informed decisions, set personal goals, and adapt to changes in their lives.

Self-Awareness and Personal Growth begin with comprehension. Understanding one's strengths, weaknesses, values, and desires is the first step toward personal growth. Comprehension enables individuals to assess their current situation and identify areas where they can improve. Whether it's emotional intelligence, mental well-being, or physical health, comprehension is the foundation of self-awareness and growth.

Making Informed Decisions is another crucial aspect of comprehension in personal life. People who understand their options and the potential consequences of their actions are better equipped to make choices that align with their long-term goals. Whether it's career decisions, relationship choices, or financial planning, comprehension ensures that individuals consider all factors before making significant life decisions.

Building Strong Relationships also depends on comprehension. Understanding others' perspectives, needs, and emotions is key to forming meaningful and lasting relationships. Comprehension of social dynamics allows individuals to communicate more effectively, resolve conflicts, and build trust. This, in turn, leads to more fulfilling personal and social lives.

Adapting to Life's Changes requires comprehension as well. Life is full of unexpected events, from career changes to personal losses. Comprehension helps individuals adapt to these changes, learn from them, and grow stronger. By understanding the challenges, they face and conceptualizing possible solutions, individuals can navigate life's difficulties with resilience and grace.

In personal life, comprehension is essential for growth, decision-making, and building meaningful relationships. It ensures that individuals can understand themselves and the world around them.

5. Comprehension for Teachers: Assessing Student Progress and Facilitating Learning: For teachers, comprehension is a critical tool in shaping how they approach their students' learning and assess their progress. Teachers need to comprehend not only the subject matter but also their students' individual learning needs, strengths, and challenges. This understanding allows them to create an effective learning environment and provide meaningful feedback.

Understanding Student Needs is essential for teachers. By comprehending the individual strengths, weaknesses, and learning styles of their students, teachers can tailor their instruction to meet each student's needs. This comprehension allows teachers to differentiate their teaching methods and provide support where it's most needed, ensuring that all students have the opportunity to succeed.

Assessment and Feedback are important components of teaching. Teachers must comprehend students' learning progress, identify areas for improvement, and provide constructive feedback. This feedback helps students understand where they are in their learning journey and how they can improve. Teachers' comprehension of students' progress enables them to adjust their teaching strategies and provide targeted support.

Encouraging Critical Thinking is another key role for teachers. Comprehension helps teachers assess how well students grasp complex concepts and apply them critically. Teachers who comprehend students' thinking processes can guide them to engage more deeply with the material and develop higher-order thinking skills.

Creating an Inclusive Classroom requires comprehension of students' diverse backgrounds, abilities, and learning styles. Teachers who comprehend the diverse needs of their students are better able to create an inclusive learning environment that accommodates different learners. This approach fosters an environment where all students feel valued and supported in their learning journey.

For teachers, comprehension is essential for effective teaching, assessment, and support. It allows them to understand their students' needs, facilitate growth, and encourage academic achievement.

Conclusion:

Comprehension is central to the 8C Appraisal Framework, influencing how individuals and organizations approach learning, decision-making, and personal development. Whether it's students comprehending academic content, employees understanding their roles, organizations navigating market dynamics, or teachers assessing student progress, comprehension plays a pivotal role in each domain.

By fostering strong comprehension skills, individuals can improve their ability to make informed decisions, solve problems, and grow in their personal and professional lives. The 8C Appraisal Framework emphasizes the importance of comprehension as a foundational skill for success, helping individuals and organizations reach their full potential through understanding and application of knowledge.

****

CHAPTER – VIII: THE POWER OF CASE STUDY ANALYSIS (8C)

Turning Real-Life Scenarios into Learning Experiences

Case studies have long been regarded as one of the most effective methods of teaching, learning, and decision-making. They present real-world situations, challenges, and solutions, allowing individuals and organizations to analyze and reflect on different scenarios. When applied within the 8C Appraisal Framework, case study analysis becomes an invaluable tool for understanding the complexities of various situations and providing actionable insights for improvement.

The 8C Appraisal Framework emphasizes the importance of understanding and evaluating the components that contribute to success in any field. It focuses on key elements such as comprehension, context, collaboration, communication, creativity, and critical thinking, which are vital for assessing performance and progress. Case study analysis within this framework provides individuals, teams, and organizations with the opportunity to break down situations, understand challenges, and devise strategies for improvement.

In this context, the 8C Appraisal Framework offers a structured approach to examining case studies that not only emphasizes understanding but also provides actionable recommendations. Whether applied to students studying a business problem, employees analyzing workplace issues, or organizations seeking to enhance their strategies, the case study method, when aligned with the 8C Appraisal Framework, fosters deeper learning and better decision-making.

1. Case Study Analysis for Students: Understanding and Applying Academic Concepts: For students, case study analysis serves as an essential tool for bridging the gap between theoretical knowledge and practical application. In academic settings, students often learn abstract concepts, but the true value of that knowledge comes when they can apply it to real-world situations. By analyzing case studies, students can gain a more profound understanding of their subjects and develop the critical thinking skills necessary for their academic success.

In the process of case study analysis, the first step for students is to thoroughly comprehend the problem or scenario presented. The 8C Appraisal Framework encourages students to apply comprehension skills to identify key facts, challenges, and opportunities within the case. This foundational step ensures that students approach the case with clarity, enabling them to define the problem accurately.

Critical Thinking and Evaluation, Once the problem is understood, students must use critical thinking to evaluate the situation. This involves questioning assumptions, analyzing the evidence presented, and considering alternative solutions. Critical thinking is a core element of the 8C Appraisal Framework, as it challenges students to move beyond surface-level understanding and delve deeper into the complexities of the case. By analyzing the situation from multiple perspectives, students can identify the most effective solutions.

Application of Knowledge, Students must also demonstrate their ability to apply the knowledge gained in their studies to solve the problems outlined in the case study. This application requires students to connect their academic learning to real-world scenarios, showcasing their ability to transfer theoretical knowledge into practical solutions. The 8C Appraisal Framework encourages students to consider the broader implications of their recommendations and ensure they align with both the facts and their academic insights.

Communication and Presentation, Lastly, students must present their findings in a clear and concise manner. The communication aspect of case study analysis in the 8C Appraisal Framework emphasizes the importance of delivering a coherent and structured argument. Whether written or oral, the ability to communicate the analysis and proposed solutions effectively is a critical skill that students must master for academic success.

For students, case study analysis within the 8C Appraisal Framework helps in refining their problem-solving skills, critical thinking, and ability to apply academic concepts to real world scenarios.

2. Case Study Analysis for Employees: Enhancing Workplace Performance: In the professional world, case study analysis is a vital tool for employees who wish to improve their work performance and contribute more effectively to their organizations. Employees are often faced with complex tasks, and analyzing case studies can help them understand how to approach similar challenges in their daily work.

Employees are frequently presented with workplace challenges, whether related to management, project execution, or interpersonal dynamics. Using the 8C Appraisal Framework, employees can analyze case studies of similar situations to understand how different variables — such as team dynamics, communication, and resource allocation — affect outcomes. Comprehension of the underlying issues is crucial for employees to gain insights into the situation and identify possible strategies for resolution.

The next step in case study analysis for employees is problem-solving. The 8C Appraisal Framework encourages employees to approach challenges with creativity and innovation. By examining how others have tackled similar problems, employees can identify best practices, innovative solutions, and alternative strategies that may be applicable to their own work. This analysis fosters a proactive mindset that is essential for employees seeking to improve their performance and add value to their teams.

Case studies often highlight the importance of collaboration in solving complex problems. Employees can learn valuable lessons about how effective teamwork and collaboration lead to success. The 8C Appraisal Framework emphasizes collaboration as a key element in analyzing case studies, encouraging employees to think about how team dynamics influence decision-making, problem-solving, and overall performance.

Finally, employees should use case study analysis as an opportunity for reflection and learning. After evaluating the case, employees must reflect on the lessons learned and apply them to their own work. The 8C Appraisal Framework encourages a continuous learning mindset, where employees not only gain insights from case studies but also use them to drive personal and professional development.

By engaging in case study analysis, employees can enhance their problem-solving skills, foster innovation, and improve their ability to collaborate effectively within teams.

3. Case Study Analysis for Organizations: Strategic Decision-Making and Growth: Organizations, both large and small, face a variety of challenges that can have significant implications for their success. Case study analysis, when applied through the lens of the 8C Appraisal Framework, can help organizations identify patterns, evaluate past performance, and devise strategies for future growth.

Strategic Planning and Evaluation, For organizations, case studies often serve as a tool for evaluating their own strategies or analyzing the successes and failures of competitors. The 8C Appraisal Framework allows organizations to comprehensively assess both internal and external factors that influence their performance. Through case study analysis, organizations can evaluate their past decisions and identify areas where they could have taken alternative actions to achieve better outcomes.

Risk Management and Innovation, In analyzing case studies, organizations can gain valuable insights into how different risks were managed or mitigated. The 8C Appraisal Framework encourages organizations to not only understand the risks presented in a case but also to assess how innovation and creative problem-solving can be used to manage these risks in their own operations. By learning from the experiences of others, organizations can improve their approach to risk management and develop more innovative solutions.

Market and Consumer Analysis, Understanding market dynamics and consumer behavior is crucial for any organization. Case study analysis helps organizations better comprehend the factors that affect consumer decisions, market trends, and industry disruptions. The 8C Appraisal Framework emphasizes the importance of evaluating these factors and understanding their broader implications on business strategies. This helps organizations stay ahead of market trends and adapt their products or services accordingly.

Learning from Successes and Failures, Organizations can gain tremendous value from analyzing both successful and failed case studies. The 8C Appraisal Framework encourages organizations to evaluate not only the factors that led to success but also the reasons behind failure. This balanced approach allows organizations to develop a more comprehensive understanding of their operating environment and make more informed decisions moving forward.

By applying case study analysis through the 8C Appraisal Framework, organizations can refine their strategies, mitigate risks, and stay competitive in their industry.

4. Case Study Analysis for People: Navigating Personal and Social Challenges: For individuals, case study analysis can be a powerful tool for personal growth and decision-making. Whether it's evaluating a personal challenge, a social issue, or a life decision, case study analysis helps people understand different perspectives and make better-informed choices.

People often face complex personal challenges, such as career decisions, relationships, or financial matters. By analyzing case studies of others who have faced similar challenges, individuals can gain insights into their own situations. The 8C Appraisal Framework encourages self-assessment and reflection, helping people evaluate their own circumstances, strengths, and weaknesses before making decisions.

Case study analysis also provides opportunities for people to build emotional intelligence by understanding the motivations, emotions, and behaviors of others. The 8C Appraisal Framework emphasizes the importance of empathy and emotional awareness when analyzing case studies, enabling individuals to approach personal and social situations with greater understanding and sensitivity.

By reflecting on the experiences of others, individuals can learn valuable lessons about how to navigate challenges and make better decisions. The 8C Appraisal Framework encourages individuals to apply the insights gained from case study analysis to their own lives, fostering personal growth and resilience.

Life is full of changes, and case study analysis helps individuals understand how others have adapted to similar transitions. Whether it's a career change, relocation, or significant life event, individuals can learn from the experiences of others and apply those lessons to their own journeys. The 8C Appraisal Framework helps individuals navigate change by emphasizing adaptability and strategic decision-making.

For individuals, case study analysis offers a structured approach to making informed decisions and navigating life's challenges with confidence and insight.

5. Case Study Analysis for Teachers: Assessing Student Progress and Improving Teaching Methods: For teachers, case study analysis plays a crucial role in assessing student progress, identifying teaching strategies, and improving instructional methods. Teachers can analyze case studies related to student performance, classroom management, and educational outcomes to enhance their teaching practices.

Understanding Student Needs and Progress, Teachers can use case studies to assess how students respond to various teaching methods, assignments, and classroom environments. The 8C Appraisal Framework encourages teachers to evaluate student progress in a comprehensive way, considering both academic achievement and personal development. Through case study analysis, teachers can gain insights into the factors that contribute to student success or failure.

Evaluating Teaching Methods, Teachers can also analyze case studies of different teaching methods to identify what works best in promoting student learning. The 8C Appraisal Framework emphasizes the importance of creativity and critical thinking when evaluating teaching methods, allowing teachers to develop innovative approaches to instruction.

Creating an Inclusive Classroom Environment, By analyzing case studies of diverse classroom settings, teachers can gain a better understanding of how to create an inclusive environment that supports all students. The 8C Appraisal Framework encourages teachers to evaluate how different teaching strategies affect student engagement, motivation, and learning outcomes.

Enhancing Teacher-Student Interaction, Case study analysis can also help teachers improve their interactions with students. By reflecting on case studies of successful teacher-student relationships, teachers can learn how to better engage with students, provide constructive feedback, and foster a positive classroom environment.

For teachers, case study analysis is a valuable tool for improving teaching practices, assessing student progress, and creating an effective learning environment.

Conclusion:

Case study analysis, when applied within the 8C Appraisal Framework, provides a structured and insightful approach to problem-solving and decision-making. Whether for students, employees, organizations, individuals, or teachers, case study analysis helps individuals and groups gain a deeper understanding of challenges, identify solutions, and make informed decisions. By reflecting on past experiences and learning from others, case study analysis empowers individuals to improve their performance and achieve their goals.

Through the lens of the 8C Appraisal Framework, case study analysis not only facilitates learning and growth but also fosters creativity, critical thinking, collaboration, and effective communication. It enables individuals to navigate complex situations and make decisions that drive personal, academic, and professional success.

This holistic approach to case study analysis, when applied to different audiences, provides valuable lessons and fosters growth across various domains. The 8C Appraisal Framework ensures that case study analysis is not just a tool for problem-solving but a catalyst for personal and professional development.

****

THE CONCLUSION: CULMINATION OF THE 8C APPRAISAL JOURNEY

A Transformational Odyssey

The journey through the 8C Framework is not merely academic or professional, it is deeply transformational. From the first step of communication to the analytical strength of case study analysis, this framework has traversed intellectual, emotional, organizational, and societal landscapes.

As we arrive at the final chapter, the purpose is not only to summarize the significance of the 8Cs but also to inspire application, innovation, and introspection. For students, employees, organizations, people at large, and teachers, the 8C Framework is a lifelong compass.

The 8C Framework is a transformative model designed to foster holistic growth across education, work, and personal development. Rooted in eight powerful principles, Communication, Configuration, Chronicle, Completeness, Conception, Cognizance, Comprehensive, and Case Study Analysis, as it serves as a blueprint for lifelong learning and performance excellence

The concluding insights will tie together every element we explored and offer direction on how to implement the 8Cs as a daily practice, leadership tool, and developmental blueprint.

1. Communication: An Evolving Dialogue:

Students can develop confidence in presenting ideas, participating in group work, and articulating academic understanding. Communication skills help them build networks and foster peer collaboration.

Employees benefit from enhanced interpersonal communication, improved reporting skills, and professional articulation that drives teamwork and customer engagement.

Organizations gain when internal and external communication is structured, transparent, and culturally sensitive, enhancing brand image and productivity.

People can resolve conflicts, express emotions, and build relationships more effectively, leading to social and emotional well-being.

Teachers use communication to explain concepts, provide feedback, and build trust, significantly impacting student performance and motivation.

2. Configuration: Designing Futures:

Students who learn to organize time, resources, and information perform better in both academics and extracurriculars.

Employees who master configuration manage workflows, prioritize tasks, and adapt to evolving roles and expectations.

Organizations achieve strategic efficiency when they design their systems, roles, and operations with flexibility and foresight.

People who configure their routines and goals experience greater balance, purpose, and fulfillment.

Teachers configure lesson plans, classroom strategies, and evaluation methods to cater to varied learner needs and educational outcomes.

3. Chronicle: Preserving Progress:

Students benefit from journaling, portfolios, and feedback logs that help them see their progress and plan improvements.

Employees who document contributions and learning demonstrate their value during appraisals and internal reviews.

Organizations that preserve institutional memory avoid redundancy, celebrate milestones, and improve continuity.

People can reflect on life events, habits, and patterns to make informed decisions and embrace personal growth.

Teachers who chronicle student development provide better mentoring and more personalized assessments.

4. Completeness: The Standard of Integrity:

Students show academic integrity and build a reputation for diligence by submitting complete, well-thought-out assignments.

Employees gain respect and trust by delivering on responsibilities with thoroughness and accountability.

Organizations that deliver complete solutions and services build long-term customer loyalty and a reputation for excellence.

People who fulfill commitments strengthen personal credibility and reliability.

Teachers instill the value of completeness by expecting full participation and detailed submissions, fostering responsibility.

5. Conception: Creating the New:

Students are encouraged to ideate and explore new perspectives, contributing to innovation within academic and real-world challenges.

Employees generate solutions, propose improvements, and innovate within their roles to drive organizational progress.

Organizations thrive on innovation and adaptability, propelled by teams that prioritize ideation and design thinking.

People can reinvent their paths by developing creative solutions for personal, social, or entrepreneurial challenges.

Teachers design innovative teaching methods, projects, and assessments to enhance learning outcomes and engagement.

6. Cognizance: Awareness that Transcends Time:

Students who understand their learning styles, strengths, and challenges become more self-regulated and motivated learners.

Employees who are self-aware improve emotional intelligence, workplace adaptability, and career trajectory.

Organizations benefit from leadership and teams that practice self-reflection, emotional intelligence, and stakeholder awareness.

People with personal cognizance make ethical decisions and foster meaningful relationships.

Teachers aware of student diversity and classroom dynamics create inclusive, responsive, and empathetic learning spaces.

7. Comprehensive: The Intelligence of Inclusion:

Students gain deeper insights when they analyze topics from multiple viewpoints and connect concepts across subjects.

Employees become effective strategists and problem-solvers when they consider organizational goals, stakeholder needs, and environmental trends.

Organizations that apply comprehensive approaches become more adaptable and inclusive in decision-making and problem-solving.

People develop balanced perspectives and avoid bias when they approach life with comprehensive awareness.

Teachers enhance learning by designing assessments and discussions that explore content deeply and from diverse angles.

8. Case Study Analysis: From Theory to Practice:

Students learn to apply knowledge to real-world scenarios, improving critical thinking and decision-making.

Employees develop sharper business acumen and contextual understanding through case-based learning.

Organizations refine strategies and practices by studying internal and external case analyses.

People understand societal patterns, personal choices, and professional development by analyzing relevant life scenarios.

Teachers enrich learning experiences by integrating case studies that connect theory to real-life applications.

What began as a list of concepts is now a dynamic map for personal and professional excellence. The 8C Framework empowers students to become intentional learners, employees to become value-driven contributors, organizations to become purpose-led systems, people to become mindful decision-makers, and teachers to become transformative guides.

Each of the 8Cs, when practiced with sincerity, leads to growth that is not only external but deeply internal. They are not goals to be checked off, but qualities to be nurtured continually. The framework encourages integration—every C enhances the effectiveness of the others. Communication fuels collaboration in configuration; cognizance deepens the impact of conception; completeness elevates the value of chronicle; and case studies tie it all together.

The time ahead belongs to those who can adapt, create, reflect, and act with purpose. The 8C Framework does not promise easy success, it promises meaningful progress. It is a call to cultivate character alongside competence, and empathy alongside efficiency.

May this final chapter not be an end but a beginning, an invitation to carry forward the 8Cs into your academic, professional, personal, and societal endeavors.

****

The 8C Appraisal Framework is not an end, but a beginning to conscious growth and purposeful transformation. Let this be your guide as you move beyond breakthroughs into a life of clarity and impact.